COMPLETE SENTENCES

Tom Snarsky

ISBN: 978-1-915079-30-5

Cover designed by Aaron Kent

Edited and typeset by Aaron Kent

Broken Sleep Books Ltd
Rhydwen,
Talgarreg,
SA44 4HB
Wales

Contents

Complete Sentences

Tom Snarsky

I Was Going To Burn Some Sage For The
People Of This World But I Read An Article
On The Internet Saying It Was A Bad Idea

Also I didn't have any sage
To burn
Doing nothing is always easier
Ask the cop in the graveyard
Or the teacher who
Every day
Parks her car in front of legions
Of Massachusetts dead
And goes to work teaching
Students about the history
Of witches thieves
And revolutionaries

Angel's Grail

Kristi's cat Maggie
died today. She was in her
teens and tired.

My kids——my students——
are in their teens and tired too.
Some of them work at

night, stressing about
money and the future. How
can I really ask

them to do their home-
work when so many other
things are pressing on

their minds? They are not
cats, free to sleep days and stalk
their way through nights like

some secret disease
that will kill you in your bed.
They are too kind and

work too hard for that.
Tomorrow I'll cancel class
for our bereavement,

even though it's Sun-
day and you don't cancel class
in high school, that's not

how it works. Instead
I'll write a poem where all my
kids write elegies

to Maggie in lieu
of the day's lesson. Then, when
one boy shares a line

comparing Maggie's
fur to the sound of waning
rainfall, I'll just cry.

Middle School

When you love wrong your world ends
Phèdre Phèdre Phèdre Phèdre
Spotlight Telemachus detachment & singing

Ted Hughes gets to the end of his life
& writes that monster book on Shakespeare
The movie *Camp* (2003) is over a decade away

American teenagers doing musicals have not yet been
Apotheosized in Ryan Murphy's *Glee*
Nor has the spotlight's murderous intent fully

Revealed itself & so we have the poet reading
Desperately uncarefully
To feel something

New after translating *Phèdre* & keeping the grave
Accent on the title character's name
Among the only Frenchisms that survive

In a limpid but maybe-too-level free
Verse version the theater feels like the right
Place for Hughes to rip the heart out of his empty

Life à la Jonathan Pryce's character's threat
To Bond in that late '90s franchise entry
With the newspaper & the BMW

The threat will be carried out by another man
In keeping with the tragic tradition
But that is less important than the unity

Across all these myriad texts in how
They *lie* sometimes musically but always
In full view of a kind of truth

The viewer gets to hold most
Of the time or touch a little at least *see* it
Though once they do it reels them in brutally

To tragedy's machine
Old mug of Zippo lighters at the antique
Store the fire going out

In Phèdre's eyes jaundiced opposite of
Rachel Berry's Anna Kendrick's aqueous spotlit
Reflection round the iris on a held note

A thin annular structure
The jaillike perimeter of the American school
I'm about to go back to teach in one soon

& all this cowardly intertextuality is
To not deal with that fact
You know what's fucked is I did everything

I would normally do at the end of last year
But I didn't help my kids make their lit mag like
I had done the year before I forgot about it almost

Completely &/so it didn't happen
It's one of the only places in school kids can lie
Freely with no trouble (nobody reads it

But them) & then they can be the reader
For every piece other than their own & feel that glimpsing itch
Like writing will continue to haunt them

Until it has unknotted itself from the inside
Of their heart & lungs which doesn't happen to everyone
Like hey Ted got stuck doing it (or maybe was cursed to do it)

Through to the end

Truth and Love

There are a million things
I should be doing right now
That aren't writing a poem
So I will write a poem

I'm using an old note
On my phone so I promise
The title is not premeditated
It's just something

One of my students said
During the usual Wednesday
Afternoon meeting of the
Malden High School

Philosophy Club it was
The start to her rejoinder
"So back to the Truth
And Love thing" we had

Been discussing the
Question "What is love"
And we could not agree
If love was closer

To Truth or Untruth
Like when Proust's
Jealous Lover thinks
Albertine is cheating or

When one student talks
About how her sister
Says she loves her
Abusive boyfriend

Even went back to him
She said how can we
Know what it's like
From the outside

(I hear this and think
About how no one would
Understand Lol Stein
If she explained herself)

And then someone else
Says sometimes even on
The inside you don't know
Like you could think

Everything's fine but
You're really hurting
The person you love or
You're calling something love

That isn't and now
We are talking about labels
Who can call what
What and two students

Gesture at my bi pride
Flag during their stories
About how they relate
To that label, what coming

Out was like for them
The munchkins are almost
Gone and we agree
We'll continue next week

Talking about labels
We haven't gotten
To the bottom of it yet
Like the laundry pile I

Should be putting away
Instead of writing this

coign of vantage

And if sun comes　　　.
How shall we greet him?
　　— Gwendolyn Brooks

it's 30 minutes until sunset
when i will post the picture i took
of "lebensweisheitspielerei"
i had been missing the things i
usually touched, including
that big unwieldy faber & faber
collected poems of wallace stevens
that lived in my car
in the center console
the way poetry could steal
a few minutes between tasks
idling in one of america's few
remaining parking lots
(hard(l)y har har)
the way touch made it more possible
to just thumb a poem
for a moment, like a protective thimble
against the blowback
of the world
its repeated needle jabs
this thimble thought brought me to
(but first i hope you check out
the wikipedia page for thimbles,
it's really the gold standard)
touch pieces, i.e.
little talismans of medicine & luck
kings & queens rubbing coins
on the heads of the sick

to heal them
(if it didn't work
then you simply were not
faithful enough)
it's a short citational road from the touch piece
to the mercury dime
famous american instance of same
the god of commerce on a coin
which of course would be the irony
here but it's even better, that the front
of the mercury dime is really meant
to be a picture of liberty
's bust, & everyone just mistook
liberty for mercury
almost as american a confusion
(freedom for the mercurial;
god just think of insurance)
as doing your own work on company time
or the brute fact of a parking lot
our flattest terraformation
if the parking lot is the actual
physical space i return to the most
for writing then the idea
-space i return to the most
in poems
is the sea
i grew up near one
& just read for the first time
greta wrolstad's
"notes on sea & shore" it showed me
how much i still have to learn
about this craft
on its open water
wikipedia is generous

with the terminology for oceans
lakes rivers all the lands
& land formations
incident to them
i learned that a ria
is not air or a song but instead
a drowned river valley
though to see something so close
to aria put me in mind of stevens
cartoonish operatic
great lover of islands
& a seller of insurance
there are so many names for cliffs
did you know "coign of vantage"
means "a favourable position
for observation or action"
funny that metal currency
reënters our ear here
& i could've sworn stevens had a poem
actually called "aria"
sharon olds sharon olds
but searching i found instead
the are-you-fucking-with-me? fact
that his wife elsie was the model
for the mercury dime
the selfsame one
an instance of which i bought
on ebay
for a dollar after the touch piece affair
i carry it with me every day now
just to see if
like the other sacred coins of lore
faithfulness helps
it to heal

mine's a '42 so i'm starting with parts
of a world the stevens book from that year
it & sharon olds both born in the same revolution
while the world was being made
violently aware
of its parts
to figure out what the fuck exactly
the universe is trying to tell me
with this confluence
not all these researches have been done
in parking lots
stevens was a role model in almost nothing
except stealing time from work to write
the french say *faire*
de la perruque literally making
of the wig
doing one's own work
on company time
i'm writing this now during a class
the kids are in their breakout rooms
i am being the worst
version of myself qua teacher
sitting on my remote little shore all helen
in egypt
my achilles a stubborn sea bird
merzbow's new album screaming dove
is out soon & not far
into parts of a world we read
"[p]oet, patting more nonsense foamed
[f]rom the sea," three lines down
from a reminder of why
stevens is such a racist disaster
called Gwendolyn Brooks a horrible name
thought mussolini should take

ethiopia & yet Gwendolyn Brooks herself casts
in 1955
the deciding vote
to give an earlier version
of the very book in my hands
the national book award
(is this true?)
the ceremony is
three months after
the murder of emmett till
sharon olds' aria for trayvon martin
po(u)ring like hot milk from the future
& whiteness lets me mark time like this
do my little historiography
of poetry & grief
& who won what award(s) & when
defer to gilded poets like stevens
or bronk who worked unfettered
in "snug unawareness" (Brooks again)
built their arks before 9
after 5
perchance between
only had sense & meaning
to worry about
were not scared of money
or property
didn't have to be
greta's poem of the sea
begins "[a]s for gold's effect
on the first white men
on this continent,
a Nahuatlan scribe said
they fingered it
as if their hearts

were illumined
[&] made new"
[my removal
of the italics]
my '42 mercury hums
from its dime bag
in my wallet
entitlement of touch
of holding
a need to seal off
from others
greta's poem continues "we
are all unmoored", sure
but the mooring of starting out
is imperfectly shared
in america of its white lines
in parking lots
its spotty healthcare coverage
& sunsets
today's instance of which
is two minutes earlier
than yesterday's
stevens's blue-green pines
bronk's blue spruces watch
the change, those
slow sentries of sun
range rover sentinel
a headline from last year reads
"[t]he market for bulletproof vehicles
is exploding" all that
ballistic steel plating
with beautiful souls inside
do you think a teacher could afford
a bulletproof car

just smudged the stevens collected's
white cover with oil grease
bc Kristi & i changed the driver rear tire
on my 2003
toyota camry
xle
the first & only car i've ever bought
with teaching money
very susceptible
to gunfire
luckily (???) with covid, remote learning
a school shooting would require
very ambitious bullets
maybe i'd be lucky
& get fired on
(say by a winchester
manufactured in new haven
the gun that won
the west)
with my mercury dime in my breast
pocket so just like with roosevelt's notes
& glasses case
i'd be ok
teach an 80-minute class after
hell, 84
this poem is now very current events
the event being one long unfurling
american violence
& the current being mitigated
by the splitting
of the ria
hopping delta islands
on a pogo stick
look carefully

it's nearly 5:55
the sunset's coming
do you see it from your little white cliff
removed from all the rushing
of the water do you see it
from your little
white cliff
do you
& if you do
if you do see it
what are you
& your shiny coin
your shiny coin
not of gold
going to do about it
about the fact that all my friends don't have
insurance, about "the regulation of
weights and rates
in the marketplace" (jack sharpless)
to which must be lent
"discerning,
personal attention"
(sharpless again)
all these poets dying young
sharpless at 38
wrolstad at 24
Brooks at 83 (still too soon)
snarsky at tbd
louise glück agreed with bonnefoy
a poet is a joke of a thing
to call yourself
you save it for your heroes
climbing their thin-limbed trees in the dark
balancing enough to report

what Brooks somewhere
calls "tender grandeur"
the golden light on the wavecrests
the purple martins
a screaming dove
about halfway through
parts of a world we have:
"[t]wo people, three horses, an ox
[a]nd the sun, the waves together in the sea"
compare the bronk
of "midsummer":
in certain pictures, envied landscapes are seen
(through a window, maybe)
like quotation marks
do you think bronk ever really found love
in his life
love subs in for art
almost naturally
in his last poem:
love isn't made; it's in the world almost
unseen but found existent there
like gentle crushes
like risk
like an ashrita furman guinness world record
for watermelons sliced
on the stomach in one minute
the tragedy of only having an emoji
for watermelon that is already sliced up
the little seeds like delta islands
amidst embarrassment
river-red

cw: trees

Two days after Jaden died
I posted a picture of a question
From the Arbor
Day Foundation Annual Survey

Do you ever relax
In the shade of a tree
Yes or No
Almost instantly

The pic got flagged
& taken down
Post removed for suicide or self-injury
I sighed, heavy, & continued

My long rehearsal
For a day without death

Acknowledgements

Many thanks to the editors at *Marías at Sampaguitas* and to Giacomo Pope at *Neutral Spaces*, for creating welcoming places where some of these poems got to exist before here.

Thanks too to Ashley Elizabeth, whose careful reading and thoughtful commentary immeasurably improved `coign of vantage'.

`cw: trees' is in memory of Jaden Brito-White.

LAY OUT YOUR UNREST

www.ingramcontent.com/pod-product-compliance
Lightning Source LLC
Chambersburg PA
CBHW031636040426
42452CB00007B/852